Weathering The Storm:
Disaster Preparedness
How To Survive The Fall Of America

By
Landra L. Muhammad

Weathering The Storm:
Disaster Preparedness
How To Survive The Fall Of America

This book provides a compilation of both original and work obtained from the internet of many authors' works that have been gathered from the public domain of the Internet over the course of many years

Contents

Word To The Wise

"I saw the earthquake in Japan and the Tsunami that followed and the damaging of nuclear reactors that began poisoning the air and the water and I began to age as I was looking at it because I knew there was a deeper significance in it that God wanted me to look into.

And when I saw the horror of the suffering of the Japanese people. As prepared as they are, as technologically proficient as they are yet, they were not prepared for the magnitude of what happened to them.

And what made me want to call a press conference was to warn America that a MAJOR Earthquake is on the way to you and me and us.

Death and Destruction is at the door of all of us and we are worse prepared than the Japanese. And the arrogance of the American Government and people to think that our nuclear reactors are secure, when two major ones are sitting on fault lines.

Much Death ... I'm gonna say it again *Much Death* is on its way.

And what is that for? Ya know, say well Farrakhan, why are you doing this?

My teacher, the Honorable Elijah Muhammad was not only a Messenger of God and more, he was a guide and warner to you black people, and to the American people and to the American Government and to the Nations of the Earth. He told us the headlines before ever we saw them. He knew what was coming....

I pray that what we see going on in the world, that we will try our best to be prepared.

You need to store some water in your homes. You need to store some food in your homes ... groceries that will allow you to be in your homes for 2 to 3 weeks or 2 to 3 months."

Minister Louis Farrakhan
March 31, 2011

Chapter 1

Why the need for Disaster Preparedness?

Disaster
noun
1. a calamitous event, especially one occurring suddenly and causing great loss of life, damage, or hardship, as a flood, airplane crash, or business failure.

Preparedness
noun
1. the state of being prepared; readiness.

Prepare
verb
1. to put in proper condition or readiness

As you can gather from the definitions above, the usage of the term "Disaster Preparedness" covers much more than a winter storm! Though a disaster can in fact come in the form of something natural, such as: tornadoes, floods, solar flares, drought, wildfires, volcanoes, temperature extremes (hot and cold), tsunamis and earthquakes.

Disasters can also be those of man-made origin, including: nuclear, chemical explosions or leaks, air-borne illnesses, biological laboratory agents, as well as structural collapses (ex:Twin Towers in NY). Not to mention, social unrest, like what was witnessed in Ferguson, Missouri. Or what about a pandemic such as an Ebola quarantine! Imagine martial law being implemented, then what are we to do?

There is another type of disaster that many people do not consider, until it happens that is, and that is a personal disaster. This type of disaster comes in the form of unemployment or diminishment of income, which may lead to loss of one's peace of mind. This is considered a disaster because you have no income to purchase food or support yourself/family. Here is something to think on, how well would you survive with chaos and violence in the streets and the inability to leave your home for even a loaf of bread because of the chaos? Again, these are types of disasters that will continue to visit America.

In the summer of 2003 there was a major software bug that spanned from Canada through Vermont, New York, New Jersey, Connecticut, Ohio and Michigan. The interesting thing was, initially nobody knew what was going on, myself included. I mean that Emergency Broadcast System, that television systems are required to occasionally test, didn't work either, nor did the radio stations. There was actually only one television station that was still broadcasting, the local Telemundo station, so if you didn't speak Spanish, you were out of luck!

Anyway, because all of the regular media was down and out, I called a sister friend of mine in Los Angeles and told her that something was happening in my neck of the woods and could she go online and find out if there were any national news reports concerning the east coast. She actually thought I was joking and laughed for a few seconds, until she saw that there was a major Power Grid Failure occurring! That night, other than my house and the neighbor a few houses down, the neighborhood was pitch black. I later found out that my neighbor had a small emergency generator in the event of blackouts.

My house was lit up like an X-Mas tree. Lights inside the house and a few extra lights that I had placed along my walkway. Ok, it may seem like a little overkill with the walkway lights, but I was expecting friends to come over asking to 'borrow' a few supplies. FYI, so anyone that asks to borrow supplies during an outage… there really is no way to borrow a candle, unless you plan on returning the used wax. (smile) The power was out for several hours and my supplies allowed me to be quite comfortable. I was able to survive with very little discomfort.

You see, even though I am originally from the Bronx; I was reared in the beautiful suburban township of Teaneck, NJ from a very young age. The side of town that I grew up in had an older model transformer, which led to many power outages that could be caused by even a small amount of rain fall. Mostly short outages of just a few hours, but looking back now, it is clear to me that this was a part of my disaster preparedness training. My parents knew that the power in the neighborhood was subject to going off so they prepared for it. There were always flashlights in the kitchen windowsill, candles above the bread basket and a portable battery operated tv and radio in the basement. Not to mention a pantry stocked with various canned foods. It was not until later in life that what my parents actions were not the norm and they probably weren't even familiar with the term Disaster Preparedness.

Hurricane Sandy, the storm left Teaneck and its surrounding communities in a huge mess. Had it not been for pre-planning, it could have been a personal mess for me as well. I, along with a few like-minded others in the community, had often gathered to discuss preparedness and 'what if' situations. This planning proved to alleviate a great deal of stress that would have come after the storm. We all remained in constant contact with each other during the storm up until the point that one by one we lost electricity. Out of our group of about 15 people, at the end of the storm only one family was left with power. Each day we all gathered at that persons home, charged our cell phones and other electronics, engaged in spirited conversation and broke bread together. Having no electricity, one my 90 something year old Great Aunts, whom had refused all of my attempts to provide her with assistance, was now delighted that I was showing up at her home with supplies in hand. And the cousin whom I stayed with during my 5 days of power outage reaped the benefits of my love of cooking as I whipped up meals for her and her friends that had all converged over to her home because she had been blessed to maintain electricity during and after the storm. The storm left amazing damage to the Northeast region; however it strengthened in many the need to prepare for the next storm.

There are several reasons people have expressed to me as to why they do not prepare for disasters. Many books have been written about "Prepping" (preparing for disasters), but I have never seen one that was specific to Black People and People of Color in general. So the question I have to ask is, "Why"? Is it because no one is concerned or is it because having a certain level of preparation is not something that Black people do? The answer in my opinion is a combination of both factors. So here is my top 7 list as to why Black People fail to prepare for disasters.

1. The United States Government, specifically FEMA (Federal Emergency Management Agency), will take care of them.

Let me express something here and in later parts of this book as well ... **FEMA IS NOT COMING TO SAVE YOU**!!! If you don't believe me, please allow me to jar your memory with the usage of two words HURRICANE KATRINA! Need I say more? I will. People atop apartment buildings: waving flags, holding signs saying 'Help Me', and video footage of dead bodies lying in the streets. I had an interesting conversation about this subject with my brother-in-law and he reminded me of an excellent point. He agreed with me that FEMA is not coming and went a little further. I'm using much less colorful words than he did (smile), but he went on to say that FEMA isn't coming, yet the National Guard is going to come to make sure that all of our black behinds stay in our own communities. My mind immediately went back to KATRINA and seeing the National Guard hovering over the people in New Orleans as well as people in the adjoining parish. Remember how they were toting guns, forcing the people attempting to flee, to return back to the disaster area?

2. This applies mostly to my Christian family that feel they are invincible because of the title of being a self-proclaimed Born Again Christian, protected by the Blood of Jesus Christ, my Lord and Saviour, thus they possess the thought and confidence that Jesus is going to come out of the sky and save his followers. As I type these words I am nodding my head in an 'I understand' manner regarding this conviction. Truly, I do understand the big picture of this thinking. I come from a very Baptist family, so I know my Christian family very well. And yes, there is an element of truth to the Jesus coming out of the sky (clouds) to save the followers, but I also know that any and all well studied Bible readers will tell you that God ALWAYS makes provisions for His Children. I think, however, Black people are missing the aspect to act upon God's warnings which He gives BEFORE His punishment and judgment is brought down. It is my belief that the Honorable Minister Louis Farrakhan is the final warner we have before the worst is yet to come!

Remember in the book of Exodus how when there was darkness upon the land, yet the Children of Israel had light? Well, they had first followed an instruction so that they might have light and food. And Noah prepared by building an ark on dry land. See how these people had to do something BEFORE the worst possible scenarios occurred i.e. final judgment and death. Now don't get me wrong, I am not claiming to be one of the prophetesses written of in scripture, but I can say that I would like to think that I am a little instrument being used by God to sound an ALERT. You can take it or let it alone.

3. My money is a little funny, so I can't afford it. In the words my father "You a damn lie." Sorry people, with 1.1 Trillion dollars in buying power, I cannot co-sign with that 'I can't afford it' statement knowing that we have money available to purchase everything else under the sun. We spend 19 million dollars a year on cell phones, 2 billion dollars on athletic shoes and to top it off, the Market research firm Mintel, states that the hair and beauty industry brings in (from black people) nearly a half trillion dollars. This includes weaves, extensions, wigs, independent beauty supply stores, distributors, e-commerce, styling tools and appliances. Believe it or not, that is more than DOUBLE the Gross Domestic Product of the country of Greece. Our free for all spending unfortunately shows a lack of priority in that which they feel is important. Hopefully by the end of this book, you will have a better understand of the importance of preparedness.

4. "My Church is going to help me". This is a piggy back of excuse number 2 and again, this is a HORRIBLE choice. In all honesty, no one is planning to save you because it is most likely that they will be busy trying to save themselves Yes I am sure that our Churches, Mosques, Synagogues and Temples would desire to help, however, most of our places of worship are barely in a position to help themselves let alone helping 'the flock' after a disaster. Let's get into the mode of thinking that we have to stop looking for others to help us.

5. "You Prepper people are crazy!" Well after watching several episodes of Doomsday Preppers, I do think that some of them are quite crazy. I am talking about the ones with underground bunkers and teaching their 9 year old daughters how to shoot AK47's. But the truth of the matter is, YOU are going to look crazy, not if, but when something happens and you don't have any food to eat. Picture yourself, out there looting and or begging for food and water.

Years ago I taught a preparedness class to a wonderful group of women and towards the end of the class with a loving, yet I'm very serious smile on my face, told them that if any of them showed up at my house within the first 72 hours after a disaster, that I would be looking at them from behind my curtain shaking my skinny little finger in a no, no, no motion and stating, May God Bless You. The one exception was if their home had been destroyed. Please know that there is a difference between sharing with your sister and brother versus being a purposeful burden. Once you have been taught you have a responsibility to do better and prepare. The days of looking for someone else to take care of you are over. Remember Matthew 25:1-13. Have your own oil because sometimes sharing is not an option.

6. "I don't know where to start". Some people mention that they are desirous of preparing; however, they see this preparation as a herculean task and are unclear as where to begin. Well, the blessing for those of you that have purchased this book, you have already overcome this issue. High 5 to you and let the prepping begin.

7. "Prepping shows that you are pessimistic". Not really, it actually shows just the opposite; that you actually believe and think about the calamities that are spoken of in books of scripture. Seeing the handwriting on the wall and not preparing is like that of an ostrich that chooses to place their heads in sand hoping and praying that the next disaster will not affect their community. Certainly, with the local and world events that we are witnessing in 2014, preparation is more and more becoming a most.

The Bible is full of passages regarding preparedness. The following Biblical and Quaranic passages does not only relate to what was rehearsed 4000 and 2000 year ago, it will and is happening in North America right NOW!

"Let Pharaoh do this, and let him appoint officers over the land, and take up the fifth part of the land of Egypt in the seven plenteous years. And let them gather all the food of those good years that come, and lay up corn under the hand of Pharaoh, and let them keep food in the cities. And that food shall be for store to the land against the seven years of famine, which shall be in the land of Egypt; that the land perish not through the famine." **Genesis 41:34-36**

"Go to the ant, thou sluggard; consider her ways, and be wise: Which having no guide, overseer, or ruler, Provideth her meat in the summer, and gathereth her food in the harvest." **Proverbs 6:6-8**

"THEN shall the kingdom of heaven be likened unto ten virgins, which took their lamps, and went forth to meet the bridegroom. And five of them were wise, and five of them were foolish. They that were foolish took their lamps, and took no oil with them; But the wise took oil in their vessels with their lamps. While the bridegroom tarried, they all slumbered and slept. And at midnight, there was a cry made, Behold, the bridegroom cometh; go ye out to meet him. Then all those virgins arose, and trimmed their lamps. And the foolish said unto the wise, Give us your oil; for our lamps are gone out. But the wise answered, saying, Not so; lest there be not enough for us and you; but go ye rather to them that sell, and buy for yourselves. And while they went to buy, the bridegroom came; and they that were ready in with him to the marriage: and the door was shut. Afterward came also the other virgins saying, Lord open to us. But her answered and said, Verily I say unto you, I know you not. Watch therefore, for ye know neither the day nor the hour wherein the Son of man cometh." **Matthew 25:1-13**

The Holy Quran also gives a strong and very direct instruction regarding preparation:

16

"… and I inform you of what you should eat and what you should store in your houses. Surely there is a sign in this for you, if you are believers." **Sura 3-48**

The title of this book is **Weathering The Storm: Disaster Preparedness How to Survive The Fall Of America**. This title is very specific, as is who it is directed to. This guidance is directed to the Children of Israel, Black People here in America and the rest of the aboriginal family Black, Brown, Yellow and Red. Yes, this book is specifically for all of you. Believe it or not, many whites, including government officials and elites are already preparing for major disasters to weather something during these last days. Of course, any sane person wants to go or come safely through a storm, danger, trouble, etc; even the wicked.

With the information contained in this book, you will have gained the knowledge to stay in your homes for at least 3 months and how to weather the effects of the various calamities that we are already beginning to witness. Along with the cycle of disaster management, this includes;

- Preparedness
- Response
- Recovery
- Mitigation

This is The Time that the books of scripture and the books of scripture is written of and is providing a piece of What MUST Be Done. I advise you to listen to Minister Farrakhan's 52 week instructional series to increase the chances of survival.

Chapter 2

Family Disaster Plan

As was discussed in Chapter 1, there are many different kinds of disasters, such as fires, floods, airplane crashes, chemical spills, pipeline leaks and explosions, which seldom give warning and can be equally devastating to their victims. So the planning you and your family do now will be of benefit for any type of disaster that can strike your community.

This family plan template will give you an easy to follow format, along with some suggestions about information you might want to include in your family disaster plan. It's not an all-inclusive list and yours will probably look different than mine, but keep in mind that this plan should be modified by you for your ever changing individual and/or family needs. You might want to use a pencil to keep the plan neat and legible, or better yet, laminate it and use dry erase markers.

At least once every 6 months have a meeting with your family to discuss and update your disaster plan with current and correct information. Determine what additional training, equipment, and supplies are needed. If your family is not as enthusiastic about planning as you are, a few weeks before your planned meeting, 'in passing' start discussing various world disasters with your family members. If they are more conscience of current disaster events, it just might stimulate their interest. At the very least it can serve as a reminder.

Lastly ... **Practice**! Occasional drills can improve reaction time and help to avoid panic and confusion in an actual emergency.

Update and review plan	Last update	Next update

Household Members

Household Members	Relation/Birth Date	Social Security Number

Household Information

Home Address: _____

Phone1: _____

Phone2:_____

E-mail 1:_____

E-mail 2: _____

Car Information

Car 1: Make _____

Model _____

Year _____

License # _____

◆•••◆

Car 2: Make _____

Model _____

Year _____

License # _____

◆•••◆

Car 3: Make _____

Model _____

Year _____

License # _____

Emergency Numbers
CALL 911 FOR EMERGENCY

Note: After a disaster, 911 may not be working. Use these numbers when able.

Fire	Phone	Address
Police	Phone	Address
Ambulance	Phone	Address
Poison Control Center	Phone	Address
Hospital Emergency Room	Phone	Address
Doctor #1	Phone	Address
Doctor #2	Phone	Address
Doctor #3	Phone	Address

Utility and Service Contacts

Water/Sewer	Phone	Address
Electric	Phone	Address
Gas	Phone	Address
Phone	Phone	Address
Cable	Phone	Address

Insurance

Policy	Name	Policy #	Phone
Health			
Auto			
Home			
Life			

Family/Friends/Neighbors

Note: Identify two neighbors. Agree to check on each other

Name: _____

Address/Location: _____

Home #: _____

Work #:_____

Cell #:_____

E-mail:_____

Name: _____

Address/Location: _____

Home #: _____

Work #:_____

Cell #:_____

E-mail:_____

◆•••◆

Name: _____

Address/Location: _____

Home #: _____

Work #:_____

Cell #:_____

E-mail:_____

◆•••◆

Name: _____

Address/Location: _____

Home #: _____

Work #:_____

Cell #:_____

E-mail:_____

Out-of-Area Contact

Name and telephone number of person outside your local area for family members to call to report their location and condition. Everyone should memorize this number! Also select an alternate contact just in case the primary contact cannot be reached.

Important: During disasters, use phone for emergencies only. Local phone lines may be tied up. Make one call out-of-area to report in. Let this person contact others.

Primary Contact Information

Name: _____

Home Address: _____

Home #: _____

Work #:_____

Cell #:_____

E-mail:_____

◆•••◆

Alternate Contact Information

Name: _____

Home Address: _____

Home #: _____

Work #:_____

Cell #:_____

E-mail:_____

●◆●●◆●

Alternate Contact Information

Name: _____

Home Address: _____

Home #: _____

Work #:_____

Cell #:_____

E-mail:_____

●◆●●◆●

Work, School, and Other Contacts

Family members should know each other's disaster procedures for work, school, or other places where they spend time during the week.

Family Member: _____

Work/School/Other: _____

Address: _____

Phone #: _____

Disaster Procedures: _____

_____

_____

_____

◆•••◆

Family Member: _____

Work/School/Other: _____

Address: _____

Phone #: _____

Disaster Procedures: _____

_____

_____

_____

◆•••◆

Family Member: _____

Work/School/Other: _____

Address: _____

Phone #: _____

Disaster Procedures:_____

_____

_____

_____

◆•••◆

Family Member: _____

Work/School/Other: _____

Address: _____

Phone #: _____

Disaster Procedures:_____

_____

_____

_____

In case of emergency, you should know if the school will keep your children until an authorized adult comes to get them. Determine what is required to release your child to your representatives if you cannot get there yourself. Update your current contact information and those people authorized to collect your children.

Reunion Procedures

Establish two places where you and your family can meet following an emergency. One immediately outside of your home, e.g. a neighbor's mailbox, for use during a home emergency **AND** another site away from home in case you can't return.

In or Around House/Apartment	Inside House/Apartment
	Outside House/Apartment
When Family is Not Home	Priority Location
	(Leave note in a designated place such as inside mailbox where you will be: i.e., neighbor, relative, park, school, shelter, etc.)

Note: Reunion and evacuation procedures need to include children at school and house members with disabilities. Talk to school officials. Write down procedures.

Important Notes and Procedures

_____

_____

_____

_____

_____

_____

_____

_____

_____

_____

_____

_____

_____

_____

_____

_____

_____

_____

Note: People with disabilities are advised to identify two or three people at work, school, neighborhood, etc. who will assist them in the event of a disaster.

Medication List

User's Name	Medication Name	Dosage/Frequency	Reason for Taking
Doctor	Prescription #	Date Started/Ending	Location of Meds

User's Name	Medication Name	Dosage/Frequency	Reason for Taking
Doctor	Prescription #	Date Started/Ending	Location of Meds

User's Name	Medication Name	Dosage/Frequency	Reason for Taking
Doctor	Prescription #	Date Started/Ending	Location of Meds

User's Name	Medication Name	Dosage/Frequency	Reason for Taking
Doctor	Prescription #	Date Started/Ending	Location of Meds

User's Name	Medication Name	Dosage/Frequency	Reason for Taking
Doctor	Prescription #	Date Started/Ending	Location of Meds

User's Name	Medication Name	Dosage/Frequency	Reason for Taking
Doctor	Prescription #	Date Started/Ending	Location of Meds

Note: Keep at least seven days of vital medications and supplies on hand. Consult with the doctor before storing medication or if you use two or more medications. Take them with you if you have to evacuate to a shelter, friend's house, or other family member's home.

Pharmacy/Doctors/Specialists

Pharmacist Name: _____

Phone #: _____

Pharmacy Name: _____

Address: _____

◆••◆

Pharmacist Name: _____

Phone #: _____

Pharmacy Name: _____

Address: _____

◆••◆

Specialist Name: _____

Phone #: _____

Organization: _____

Address: _____

Area of Concern: _____

◆••◆

Specialist Name: _____

Phone #: _____

Organization: _____

Address: _____

Area of Concern: _____

◆••◆

Specialist Name: _____

Phone #: _____

Organization: _____

Address: _____

Area of Concern: _____

◆••◆

Specialist Name: _____

Phone #: _____

Organization: _____

Address: _____

Area of Concern: _____

Additional Medical Information

Allergies to Medications	
Person's Name:	Medication:
Person's Name:	Medication:
Person's Name:	Medication:
Person's Name:	Medication:
Person's Name:	Medication:

Health/Disability Information	
Person's Name:	Information:
Person's Name:	Information:
Person's Name:	Information:

Special Needs, Equipment, and Supplies

Person's Name:	Information:
Person's Name:	Information:
Person's Name:	Information:
Person's Name:	Information:
Person's Name:	Information:

Note: Fill this and all sections out in pencil. Update regularly. If additional information is needed, tape or staple another sheet of paper.

Home Layout/Diagram

Draw a floor plan of your home showing the location of exit doors and windows, utility shutoffs, first aid kit, and emergency supplies. Make sure that *EVERYONE* in your household is familiar with it. Additionally show it to babysitters and house guests when you're going away.

Utility Control

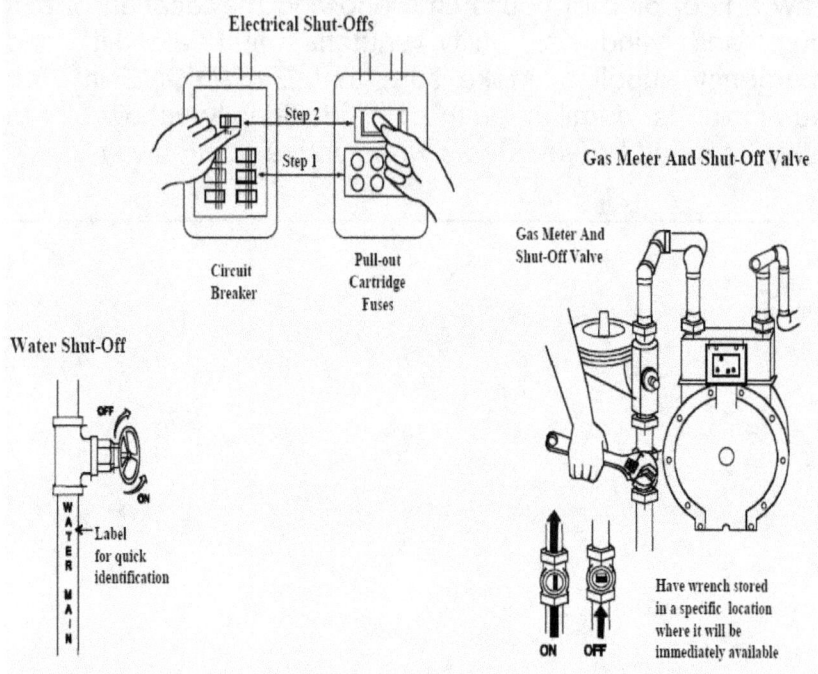

Electrical Shut-Offs

Step 2

Step 1

Circuit Breaker

Pull-out Cartridge Fuses

Gas Meter And Shut-Off Valve

Gas Meter And Shut-Off Valve

Water Shut-Off

OFF

ON

Label for quick identification

WATER MAIN

ON   OFF

Have wrench stored in a specific location where it will be immediately available

Locate each of these utility control points in your home.

Electricity: In the event that you need to turn off the electricity in your house, go to the breaker box and do the following:

    1. Turn off smaller breakers one by one
    2. Flip the "main" breaker to off last
To reenergize your home, reverse the steps above

Water: In the event you need to shut water off inside your home, find the main water valve and turn it to your right. To open the flow of water back into the house, turn it to your left.

Gas: IMPORTANT – Only turn off your gas at the meter if you smell gas!

To turn off natural gas in your house, take a wrench and tighten it on to the quarter turn valve that is on the pipe that feeds into the gas meter. Turn it one quarter turn to make the indicator parallel to the ground. In most locations, once you do this you cannot turn the gas back on to the house without the utility company.

Propane: If you live in an area that uses outdoor propane or LPG you will find this outside the home. Open the top of the tank and you will see either a regular turn knob or a quarter turn valve. Turn the knob to your right to shut off the flow of propane into your house. For quarter turn valve see above.

Practice Your Plan

Once you have developed your plan, you need to practice and maintain it. Practicing your plan will help your family instinctively take the appropriate actions during an actual emergency; even in the middle of the night. You should review your plan at least annually and make updates as necessary.

- **Quiz your children every six months so they remember what to do, meeting places, phone numbers, and safety rules.**
- **Conduct fire and emergency evacuation drills at least twice a year.** Practice driving your evacuation routes so each driver will know the way. Select alternate routes in case the main evacuation route is blocked during an actual disaster. Mark your evacuation routes on a map; keep the map in your disaster supplies kit. Remember to follow the advice of local officials during evacuation situations. They will direct you to the safest route, away

from roads that may be blocked or put you in further danger.

- **Replace stored food and water every six months.** Replacing your food and water supplies will help ensure freshness.

- **Use the test button to test your smoke alarms once a month.** The test feature tests all electronic functions and is safer than testing with a controlled fire (matches, lighters, or cigarettes). If necessary, replace batteries immediately. Make sure children know what your smoke alarm sounds like.

- **If you have battery-powered smoke alarms, replace batteries at least once a year.** Some agencies recommend you replace batteries when the time changes from standard daylight savings each spring and again in the fall. "Change your clock, change your batteries," is a positive theme and has become a common phrase.

- **Replace your smoke alarms every 10 years.** Smoke alarms become less sensitive over time. Replacing them every 10 years is a joint recommendation by the National Fire Protection Association and the U.S. Consumer Products Safety Commission.

- **Check your fire extinguisher to ensure it is properly charged.** Fire extinguishers will not work properly if they are not properly charged. Use the gauge or test button to check proper pressure. Follow manufacturer's instructions for replacement or recharging fire extinguishers. If the unit is low on pressure, damaged, or corroded, replace it or have it professionally serviced.

Chapter 3

Survival Kits

A survival kit is a collection of items that you will need after a disaster has occurred, that will aid in your safety and survival. When you have survived a major disaster the first 72 hours are most critical. Chances are great that you will need to fend for yourself without the assistance of authorities or response services. Even if there are response teams in the close vicinity, they may not be able to reach you. And often emergency response services will be dealing with other larger scale situations, such as fires, building collapses

You never know where you will be when disaster strikes so it is very important to have survival kits in various locations. There are different types of survival kits for each location and here are some reasons why you will need to have each of them, followed by an actual checklist to help you prepare.

Shelter in Place

Is the use of a structure and its indoor atmosphere to temporarily separate individuals from a hazardous atmosphere. Quite simply, it means, stay put where you are! Now that does not mean if you are standing in the kitchen or in the garage to stay there. It means to stay in the safest part of the house or office where you are currently at. More on this will be discussed in chapter 5.

Because the Honorable Minister Louis Farrakhan advised us to have enough food and supplies to stay in our homes for a period of time, it is very important to discuss the subject of Sheltering in Place in depth. Some of these items have been mentioned previously, but they are all worth reiterating. The following is a list of procedures which can aide in our safety.

- Stay inside the enclosed building or your "safe room".

- Close and lock all windows and doors to the outside. Close drapes and shades over all windows. Push wet towels under the doors to help seal against outside air if appropriate.
- Turn off all heating/air conditioning systems, and switch inlets or vents to the "closed" position. Extinguish fireplace fires and close dampers.
- In the "safe room" – use tape and pre-cut/labeled plastic sheeting to seal around doors, window, heating vents, skylights, or any opening which could let air in.
- Seal bathroom exhaust fans or grills, range vents, dryer vents, and other openings (in "safe room" only).
- If there isn't a phone in your designated shelter room, bring along a battery-operated or cellular phone.
- Listen to the Emergency Alert System radio messages and follow the instructions. Other local stations may carry the instructions as well.
- Do not go outside or attempt to drive unless specifically told to do so. Evacuation procedures may vary based on any danger zone areas.
- Once the emergency has passed, ventilate your entire house.

Remember that your Shelter In Place preparations complement your other family emergency preparedness efforts, and are a separate kit. Here are a few Shelter In Place don'ts:

- Don't call the school to try to pick up your children. They will be safer Sheltering-In-Place at the school than they would be riding in your vehicle. Also: the school may be outside of the hazard area – depending upon the emergency. **YOU SHOULD HAVE BEEN HOMESCHOOLING IN THE FIRST PLACE**

- Don't leave your safe room until the "all clear" signal is sounded
- Don't call 9-1-1 for a non-emergency.
- Don't wait until the disaster strikes to prepare… IT'S NEVER TOO EARLY!

Evacuation

This occurs when you are asked to leave from your current location. This can happen while at your home or in a public location such as shopping mall. For our purpose, we are discussing the need to leave your home. Just a note, because evacuation is not always the safest option in the event of a hazardous material or other similar type emergency, sheltering in place such as in your home, workplace, church or mosque would be the first choice to provide a safe haven from an emergency. But again, up-front preparations are a must.

Go Bags

72 hour bag – Go bag – Bug Out Bag, it goes by many different names, but it really is one and the same; a backpack, or some other type of bag that contains a few basic supplies that can help you immediately after a disaster. These basic items should include Food, Clothing and Shelter. Having a back-pack like Dora's or better yet the bag that Hermione Granger from Harry Potter had would be ideal, just not realistic. For those that don't understand what I am talking about, each of their bags contained EVERYTHING that you can imagine, including a kitchen sink!

Survivalweekly.com gives a wonderful understanding of the differences between an Evacuation bag and a Go-Bag. Please read: "Difference between evac bag and go-bag. The Bug-Out Bag is a stash of supplies one would keep at work, in their vehicle, or carry with them when traveling. The theory is to have on hand enough supplies to get you *from* wherever you happen to be *to* your home, retreat, or other safe location. Food, water (and the means to purify found water), comfortable walking shoes/boots, and season appropriate walking clothes are a few of the important contents of a BOB. Generally speaking, envision some type of disaster occurring when you are at work or traveling. What would you need to have with you to make it back home, assuming that for whatever reason you are forced to make that trip by foot? How long might such a trip take?

The Evacuation Kit (a.k.a. Get Out of Dodge kit, Go Bag) is different in that it presumes you are home and are forced to vacate the area for an undetermined period of time. Much of the contents of this kit will be similar to a BOB. The additions would include copies of important papers (insurance policies, bank account information, list of emergency contacts, etc.), small toiletry kit, extra clothes, and perhaps small books or toys for any kids. The idea here is you are grabbing this bag on your way out the door and heading to a motel, an emergency shelter, or a friend's/relative's home for the duration of the emergency."

Vehicle

Remember watching the news during the winter of 2011 as hundreds of people were in Chicago stuck in their cars, running out of gas and without food? Lake Shore Drive is normally a beautiful scenic road that runs near Lake Michigan, but because of a blizzard was turned into a frozen parking lot. Imagine how hungry, cold and thirsty the drivers must have been.

Even more recent is Atlanta. That simple ice storm shut down the entire city, leaving major highways impassable and students stranded.

Work

Ok, so maybe you are thinking that being stranded at work would not be too bad because there are vending machines, but think about it – do those machines store enough snacks to feed all of the employees in the building? And do you really want to make a meal of snickers bars? Continue reading to find out which items you should keep in your desk.

School

Yes, even your children should have a kit located at school. If you think that is a little overboard, please remember January of 2014. Due to severe winter weather conditions the city of Atlanta shut down and hundreds of children were stuck at school.

Well, having a school kit might not bring them home any more quickly, but it certainly can assist in keeping them calm. For various reasons, sometimes schools can get locked down. This is another reason that you should have a small kit for your child at school.

- Water (these emergency pouches may be hard for your little ones to open so if you can, stick a small water bottle in)
- Protein Snack or Granola bar (or both)
- Small flashlight or headlamp
- Emergency Whistle (and don't skimp on this — cheap whistles often don't work or are not strong enough to be heard in a lot of noise. We made that mistake when we first created our kits and found out they just don't work when needed).
- Cell phone
- Small first aid kit – and the knowledge on how to use what you've enclosed.
- Emergency Blanket
- Extra health-related items your child uses
- Hard candies for comfort & energy
- Comfort item (small stuffed animal or toy to bring comfort in crisis)
- Photo album – you can create a small photo album for your child to have photos of the family to help bring them comfort. It is also a great ID item in the chaos of pick up afterward, to have a photo of you with them for rescue workers to help expedite release to the appropriate guardian)
- Wipes – we put a small package of wipes to help keep them clean

These items can be placed in a Ziplock bag and then inside of your child's back pack. Please remind your children that this kit is NOT A TOY and not to be snacked on when they are simply a little hungry. Because of the severity of this kit, it is mentioned twice in this chapter. Our children are a great gift that many of us have been given and must do all that we can do to protect them. A hint to the wise is sufficient.

Shelter In Place List

Staples
- ☐ 1 gallon of commercially bottled water per person daily
- ☐ Canned, plastic and tetra pack juices
- ☐ Ready-to-eat canned meats, fruits and vegetables
- ☐ Soups
- ☐ Protein or fruit bars
- ☐ Dry cereal, granola or trail mix
- ☐ Dried fruit
- ☐ High energy foods such as sunflower and pumpkin seeds
- ☐ Vitamins
- ☐ Food for infants
- ☐ Honey
- ☐ Comfort/stress foods such as chocolate
- ☐ Drink mixes
- ☐ Condensed milk
- ☐ Powdered milk
- ☐ Infant care supplies
- ☐ Disposable plates, cups and utensils
- ☐ Cooking tools and fuel
- ☐ First Aid Kit with mosquito repellent
- ☐ Prescription Medicine (min. 1 week's supply)
- ☐ Prescription eyewear and contact lens solutions
- ☐ Specialty items for elderly or disabled family members such as hearing aid batteries
- ☐ Flashlights and extra batteries
- ☐ Battery operated radio and clock
- ☐ Battery operated tv
- ☐ MP3 Player
- ☐ Manual can opener
- ☐ Matches in a waterproof container

Sanitation
- ☐ Water purification kit or bleach (4 drops per qt)
- ☐ Plastic sheeting and duct tape

- ☐ Toiletries and personal hygiene items, including feminine supplies
- ☐ Soap and hand sanitizer or moist towelettes
- ☐ Toilet paper
- ☐ Disinfectant and chlorine bleach
- ☐ Plastic trash bags and plastic ties

Additional Items
- ☐ Fire extinguisher
- ☐ Wrench or pliers to turn off utilities
- ☐ Work gloves
- ☐ Complete change of clothing, including a long-sleeved shirt, long pants, socks and sturdy shoes
- ☐ Pillows, blankets, sleeping bags and towels
- ☐ Cash in small denominations and change
- ☐ Whistle to signal for help
- ☐ Dust mask
- ☐ Local maps
- ☐ Copies of important family documents in a waterproof, portable container
- ☐ Books, games, puzzles and other activities for children
- ☐ Kitchen accessories and cooking utensils
- ☐ Extra set of car and house keys
- ☐ Small shovel
- ☐ Plastic bucket with tight lid

Keep items in airtight plastic bags and put your entire disaster supply kit in one or two easy-to-carry containers such as a bucket, garbage bin, camping backpack or duffel bag.

This is a basic list. Please feel free to add items that are needed by your family.

Evacuation - How To Prioritize Your Grab and Go List

1. On the page 54, you are asked to list the most important items you want to take with you. Just brainstorm and start writing.

2. Then divide the big list into four smaller lists; what you would take if you had 5 minutes, 15 minutes, 30 minutes or 1 hour to evacuate.

3. Then arrange your items within those smaller lists in the order you would grab them in your home to save the most time. Perhaps start upstairs, and work your way down. If you don't have an upstairs, then choose a room you would go to first.

4. Gather from more than one list if you have time. For instance, if you end up with 15 minutes to evacuate, then grab items on both the 5 minute list and the 15 minute list based on location. Or if you have 30 minutes, grab from the 5 minute list, the 15 minute list and the 30 minute list. And so forth.

5. You may need to move some items to a more central location.

6. Practice the evacuation with your family. Does your teenage daughter know what an external hard drive is? Or where the 72-hour kits are?
Adjust the order of items if necessary. Teach teens that it may be safer to just get out of the house without grabbing anything.

7. Make several copies of the list and hang in various locations in your home where others will see it.

8. During an evacuation, grab the list and carry it with you as you gather items. You may want to grab a laundry basket and fill it up.

9. Also, decide on several meeting places. Consider one a mile away, one 15 miles away, one 30 miles away and one out of state.

Learn to keep your car tank full

Secure and lock your home

Listen to radio for instructions

Let others know where you are going

Grab & Go Items

List the item and where it is located. Possible ideas: Pre-packed Survival Kit, Purse, Photo Albums, Family Heirlooms, Laptop, External Hard Drive, Extra set of Car Keys, etc.

1._____

2._____

3._____

4._____

5._____

6._____

7._____

8._____

9._____

10._____

11._____

12._____

13._____

14._____

15._____

Prioritized Grab & Go List

5 Minutes	15 Minutes (add these)	30Minutes (add these)	1 Hour (add these)
STOP and GO!!!	STOP and GO!!!	STOP and GO!!!	STOP and GO!!!

Go Bag Kit List

- ☐ Flashlight
- ☐ Radio – battery operated (crank is better)
- ☐ Batteries
- ☐ Whistle
- ☐ Dust mask
- ☐ Pocket knife
- ☐ Emergency cash in small denominations and quarters for phone calls
- ☐ Sturdy shoes, a change of clothes, and a warm hat
- ☐ Local map
- ☐ Water
- ☐ Nonperishable Food
- ☐ Permanent marker, paper and tape
- ☐ Photos of family members for re-identification purposes
- ☐ List of emergency point-of -contact phone numbers
- ☐ List of allergies to any drug (especially antibiotics) or food
- ☐ Copy of health insurance and identification cards
- ☐ Extra prescription eye glasses, hearing aid or other vital personal items
- ☐ Prescription medications and first aid supplies
- ☐ Toothbrush and toothpaste
- ☐ Extra keys to your house and vehicle
- ☐ Any special-needs items for children, seniors or people with disabilities.
- ☐ Emergency Blanket

This is a basic list. Please feel free to add items that are needed by your family.

Car Kit List

- [ ] 1 large Container {With Lid}
- [ ] Change of clothes {Shirt, pants, Hoodie & Socks} for every family member
- [ ] Water bottles
- [ ] Comfy shoes/boots
- [ ] Small blanket
- [ ] Flash lights & Batteries
- [ ] Hand sanitizer
- [ ] Wet wipes
- [ ] First aid kit {Rubbing alcohol}
- [ ] Pack of Band-Aids
- [ ] Toiletries {Feminine products, toilet paper, deodorant, toothbrush & toothpaste}
- [ ] Hair brush with portable mirror
- [ ] Hand soap & Small towel {Or paper towels, napkins}
- [ ] Trash bags
- [ ] Lighter
- [ ] Granola bar or energy bar {Get at least 2 or more for each family member} Also I would get the plain ones and not chocolate as it might melt and you don't want that!
- [ ] Non-perishable food that you currently eat {Apple sauce, canned fruit}
- [ ] Small Propane or Butane Stove
- [ ] Mess Kit
- [ ] Cash & coins {in a zip lock bag}
- [ ] Scissors/ Razor blade or a pocket Knife
- [ ] Reading glasses /Contacts {If you wear them}
- [ ] Medications {Make sure to rotate them}
- [ ] Phone charger
- [ ] Small toys for you little ones {If something happens this should entertain them for a bit}
- [ ] Jumper Cables, Tire Jack
- [ ] Blanket

Do NOT store foods in your car that you do not normally eat.
If you are stuck in your car, you will need as many comforting items as possible.

This is a basic list. Please feel free to add items that are needed by your family.

Work (Get Home Bag)

- ☐ Backpack
- ☐ Food
- ☐ Water
- ☐ Reflective Tape
- ☐ Poncho
- ☐ Space Blanket
- ☐ Whistle
- ☐ COMFORTABLE WALKING SHOES (Sneakers)
- ☐ Socks
- ☐ First Aid Kit
- ☐ Flashlight
- ☐ Map of the city
- ☐ Emergency Contact Numbers
- ☐ Face Mask
- ☐ Battery operated Phone Charger
- ☐ Cash (small bills)
- ☐ Tissues
- ☐ Small Radio
- ☐ House Key (Unidentified)

This is a basic list. Please feel free to add items that are needed by your family.

School Kit List

- ☐ Water
- ☐ Granola Bar
- ☐ Flashlight
- ☐ Cell Phone
- ☐ Whistle
- ☐ Small First Aid Kit
- ☐ Emergency Blanket
- ☐ Candy (comfort)
- ☐ Comfort Item

This is a basic list. Please feel free to add items that are needed by your family.

Chapter 4

Josephs' Storehouse

Because of his gift of dream interpretation, the Biblical Joseph prepared his nation for seven years of famine after having lived through seven years of abundance. After he and the people prepared for famine, they had so much grain (food) that during the time of famine, Joseph opened the storehouses which was able to feed people from across the land.

"When the famine had spread over the whole country, Joseph opened all the storehouses and sold grain to the Egyptians, for the famine was severe throughout Egypt. And all the world came to Egypt to buy grain from Joseph, because the famine was severe everywhere." **Genesis 56-57**

We don't realize the effects of climate change and other pandemic concerns that both threaten our food supplies as well as cause increase in prices. These changes are occurring before our very eyes and we don't even realize that we are already in the beginning stages of famine. For example let's take a look at how various weather conditions have raised the prices of certain foods.

In the article The 10 Fastest Rising Food Prices written by Alexander E.M. Hess and Thomas C. Frohlich dated on April 17, 2014 states "In recent years, drought in the western U.S. has driven up the prices of meat, dairy, fruit and vegetables. Parts of California, the Southwest, and the Great Plains have suffered from three consecutive years of drought, according to Brad Rippey, meteorologist for the U.S. Department of Agriculture (USDA). More than two-thirds of California is currently covered by extreme drought, according to the U.S. Drought Monitor.

Of course, drought directly impacts crops. "Agriculture uses about 80% of California's water," Rippey told 24/7 Wall St., and because of cutbacks in water delivery, "a lot of fields may have to lay fallow."

Drought has also driven up meat prices because it caused feed prices to spike in recent years, Rippey added. The higher feed prices increase the cost of raising cattle for slaughter and, in the end, the meat prices for consumers." We are being conditioned to simply accept the price increases without a full understanding of causes. "

It is now time for all of us to follow Joseph's principals of survival during these; the harshest times that we can expect to see, not in ancient Egypt but here and now during the Fall of America.

We can become the collective Joseph of today. Let us now fill our homes with food storage that we may have a multitude of storehouses. For instance, specific designated church's, mosque and family homes full of sustenance for friends and loved ones. This concept can be expanded upon to form networks of people working together and will be discussed further in chapter 8.

The Utah State Extension Office stresses the importance of food storage as "Proper food and water storage can assist families in case of a disaster. When a disaster strikes it may be impossible to obtain food and water, even at the supermarket. Therefore, it is important to have adequate food storage and water available in case of a disaster. FYI.... In case you are wondering why I referenced the state of Utah, it is because many Mormons live in Utah and they are extremely preparedness savvy.

There are primarily two types of Food Storage: Short Term Storage and Long Term Food Storage. Your Long Term Storage items might include: Wheat, White Rice, Corn,

Sugar, Oats, Pasta, Potato Flakes, and Apple Slices which can last up to 30 years. Carrots and Powdered Milk can last for 20 years if properly stored.

Short Term Storage is your 3 month supply and could include items from your 72 hour bags and an extra supply of foods that your family eats on a weekly basis. My short term supply includes items such as roasted chilies, crushed tomatoes, tortillas and onions. These are all staple items for my family and can make up a quick Mexican influenced meal.

Now there are different methods which you can utilize to maintain your store food, such as:

- **Fresh**
- **Frozen**
- **Dehydrated**
- **Freeze Dried**
- **Canned**

Most people are familiar with Fresh, Frozen and Canned foods (more on canned foods is available in Chapter 8) however, Dehydrated and Freeze Dried are more of an advanced food storage item. Dehydration is simply the process of removing water from the food. And Freeze Drying is a dehydration process as well, the difference is that the process allows the food to become much drier, which in turn makes the food last longer.

Cooking Equipment

Now let's review some basic kitchen equipment, but remember, these utensils must be manual. And water usage is always a factor … it takes water to wash these utensils.

- Egg Beater
- Multi-Purpose Mill

- Coffee Grinder
- Food Mill
- Hand Crank Blender
- Wheat Grass Juicer

Can Opener

In my James Brown voice, I am writing **PLEASE-PLEASE-PLEASE** … do not forget to have several can openers!!! If one breaks, you will always have that back up.

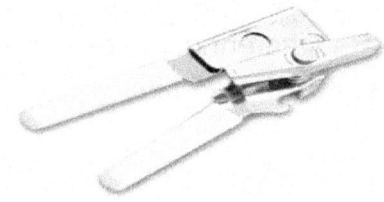

Cooking Methods

Additionally, here are a few proven methods of cooking food without the usage of electricity. Remember, this book is being written in a manner and in the format of a worst case scenario. Imagine having your food supply in order and no method to cook it. That would be a **DISASTER**!!!

Gas

Pros:
5-10 Years storage life
Relatively Inexpensive
Easy to Light and Burn

Cons:
Volatile
Priming Required
Highly Flammable

Butane Stove

Pros:
Relatively easy to find
Convenient
Clean Burning
Easy lighting, no Priming, no Pumping
Long Storage Life
Can use Indoors

Cons:
Freezes at low temperatures
Relatively expensive

Propane

Pros:
Relatively Inexpensive
Easy to Find, Buy-able in Bulk
Burns easily and hot
Can be used indoors
Stores Indefinitely

Cons:
Burns dirty
Has an odor
Priming required
Can clog stove parts

Heat Retention

Hay Box Cooker

Heat Retention

Wonder Oven

Heat Retention

Ice Box Cooker

Pros:

Thermal or Heat Retention Cooking by far are the best choice for city dwellers! Being that electricity will probably not be available, the short usage of butane, propane or kerosene stoves to bring the food to a boil, then covered with the heat retention method will allow for continued cooking. The aromas of the food can also be somewhat contained with Thermal/Heat Retention Cooking.

Sterno Stove

Pros:
Inexpensive
Cooks small amounts of food

Cons:
Short burning span

Propane Stove

Pros:
Relatively Inexpensive
Readily available
Stores Indefinitely
Rotten egg smell alerts you to possible leak

Cons:
Can explode at ignition source
If leaking, gas can accumulate and explode

Fire Wood / Fireplace

Pros:
Free if you collect/chop your own
No Toxic Fumes
Typically readily available

Cons:
Low burn efficiency
Lots of space needed for storage

Solar

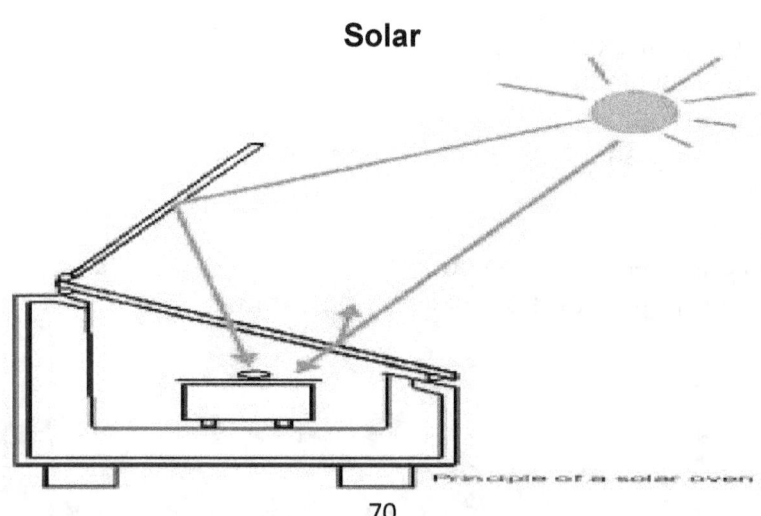

Principle of a solar oven

Solar Box

Pros:

Insulated box-in-a-box

Glass lid pointed towards the sun, traps heat inside like a greenhouse.

Food in dark covered pots reaches cooking temperatures: 300º- 450º F.

Solar

Solar Panel

Pros:

A Reflective Panel that directs sunlight to a dark-colored pot enclosed in a oven bag.

Food cooks at low heat 200º-275º F.

Folds flat, lightweight

Least expensive solar cooker.

Solar

Parabolic Cooker

Pros:

Use a parabolic mirror to focus light on a cooking pot.
The pot is placed at the focal point where the temperature
can reach over 600° F.

Most Expensive Solar Cooker

There are several types of Solar Cooking, and pending you
have a sunny day, I feel that this is the BEST METHOD of
cooking. *** If you live in the desert such as Phoenix ... this
is an ideal method for you, and you MUST practice these
methods NOW, so that you will know what you do later ***

Recipes

Lastly, here are a few recipes that you can easily
prepare with your food storage and one of the above
powerless cooking methods. My suggestion here is to
practice one or more of these recipes now – before a
disaster happens.

Navy Bean Burger

1 Pint Home canned Navy Beans, drained and rinsed
¼ cup dehydrated green bell pepper
¼ cup dehydrated onions
3 cloves garlic, peeled
1 tbsp powdered egg
1 tbsp chili powder
1 tbsp cumin
1 tsp Thai chili sauce or hot sauce
½ cup bread crumbs

1. In a medium bowl, mash navy beans with a fork until thick and pasty.
2. Using a hand held blender, finely chop bell pepper, onion, and garlic. Then stir into mashed beans.
3. In a small bowl, stir together egg, chili powder, cumin, and chili sauce.
4. Stir the egg mixture into the mashed beans. Mix in bread crumbs until the mixture is sticky and holds together. Divide mixture into four patties.
5. Cook about 8 minutes on each side. If baking, place patties on baking sheet, and bake about 10 minutes on each side.

Salmon Croquettes
1 cup water
½ cup flour
1/3 cup water
1 small jar pimentos
½ cup dried or freeze dried onion
¼ cup dried chives
½ cup mayonnaise
2 tbsp lemon juice
½ tsp seasoned salt
3 cups dry bread crumbs
4 cans (6 oz.) Skinless Boneless Salmon
1/4 cup oil

*½ cup egg replacer if flour binder is not used

1. In a small bowl rehydrate onion and chives with 1/3 cup of water.
2. In a separate bowl combine well drained pimentos, rehydrated onions and chives, mayonnaise, lemon juice and seasoned salt. Taste and adjust seasonings to personal preference.
3. Stir in 4 TBS of flour based binder, well drained salmon, and 1/2 cup of bread crumbs.
4. Divide and form mixture into 6 – 8 balls.
5. Flatten into cakes and dredge in the remaining bread crumbs.
6. Fry cakes in oil over medium low heat, 3-4 minutes per side.
7. Combine all ingredients for Lemon Herb Mayonnaise and serve along with salmon cakes.
8. *Make the flour based binder
9. Start a medium pot of water boiling and whisk together flour and 1 cup water. Once the water in the pot is boiling, reduce heat to low and pour mixture into a double boiler over top of the pot to cook. Cook mixture just until thick and remove from heat.
10. Whisk until smooth and then add 1 TBS oil and 1/8 tsp. salt. Set aside until binder is needed.

Southwestern White Chili
1 cup onion, chopped (¼ cup dehydrated onions)
4 cloves garlic, minced
2 tsp ground cumin
1 t. dried oregano, crushed
¼ tsp ground red pepper
3 15.5 oz cans navy beans, drained and rinsed or 1 lb.
2 ½ cup. navy beans, cooked and rinsed
2 4 oz cans diced green chili peppers
4 cups chicken broth
3 cups cooked chicken, chopped
2 cups shredded Monterey Jack cheese (8ounces)

Sour Cream (dehydrated)

1. In a 3 1/2 to 6-quart pot, place the onion, garlic, cumin, oregano, red pepper, beans, chili peppers, broth and cooked chicken. Stir to combine.
2. Cover and cook on low heat for 2 hours. Stir in the cheese until melted.
3. Ladle the chili into 8 bowls. If desired, top with sour cream and sprinkle with additional chili peppers or chives.

*Landra's Note – This is a perfect meal to prepare in your Solar Oven.

Baked Spinach Stuffed Shells
1 Pint Home canned Tomato Sauce
Cooking spray
2 ½ cops ricotta cheese
½ cup. (2 ounces) dried Parmesan cheese
½ tsp onion powder
½ t. dried oregano
¼ tsp salt
¼ tsp freshly ground black pepper
1 can spinach, chopped thawed, drained, and squeezed dry
1 tbsp powdered eggs
1 garlic clove, minced
24 cooked jumbo pasta shells

1. Spread ½ cup Marinara over bottom of a 13 x 9-inch baking dish coated with cooking spray.
2. Combine ricotta and next 8 ingredients (through garlic) in a large bowl, stirring well.
3. Spoon about 1 1/2 tablespoons filling into each pasta shell. Arrange stuffed shells in prepared dish; spread with remaining 1 1/2 cups Basic Marinara.
4. Cover and bake at 350° for 30 minutes. Let stand 5 minutes before serving.

Vegetable Curry

2 tbsp oil
1 large yellow onion, finely diced
4 medium cloves garlic, minced
One 2-inch piece fresh ginger; peeled and finely grated (1 Tbs.) (or 1 tsp dried ginger)
1 tbsp ground coriander
1 ½ tsp ground cumin
3/4 tsp ground turmeric
1/2 tsp. cayenne
1 tbsp tomato paste
2 cups chicken broth or vegetable broth (or 2 cups water and 2 bouillon cubes)
1 cup light coconut milk
One 3-inch cinnamon stick
Fine sea salt and freshly ground black pepper
Vegetables of your choice equaling the following:
One 15 ½ oz string beans or 1 pint home canned
One 15 ½ oz potatoes or 1 pint home canned
One 15 ½ oz stewed tomatoes or 1 pint home canned
One 15 ½ oz can carrots or 1 pint home canned
One 15 ½ oz can navy beans, drained or 1 pint home canned
One 15 ½ oz can spinach or (4 lightly packed cups if you have fresh from your garden)
2 tbsp lime juice
1 tsp finely grated lime zest
1 ½ tsp dried cilantro

1. In a 5- to 6-quart Dutch oven or other heavy-duty pot, heat the oil over medium-high heat.
2. Add the onion and cook, stirring occasionally, until beginning to brown, 3 to 4 minutes. Reduce the heat to medium (or medium low if necessary) and cook until the onion is richly browned, 5 to 7 minutes more.
3. Add the garlic and ginger; cook, stirring, for 1 minute to blend the flavors.

4. Add the coriander, cumin, turmeric, and cayenne; stir for 30 seconds to toast the spices.
5. Add the tomato paste and stir until well blended with the aromatics, about 1 minute.
6. Add the broth, coconut milk, cinnamon stick, 1 tsp. salt, and 1/4 tsp. pepper and bring to a boil. Reduce the heat to medium low or low and simmer for 10 minutes.
7. Add the string beans, potatoes, tomatoes, and carrots.
8. Raise the heat to medium high and return to a boil.
9. Reduce the heat to medium low, cover, and simmer until the vegetables are tender, 20 to 25 minutes. Discard the cinnamon stick.
10. Stir in the beans, spinach, lime juice, and zest; cook about 3 minutes more.
11. Salt to taste. Serve garnished with the cilantro.

Wheat Bread
1 ¼ cup warm water
1 tbsp yeast
1 tbsp white vinegar
¼ cup honey or ½ cup sugar
2 ¾ cups. whole wheat flour
¼ cup wheat gluten
1 t. salt
2 tbsp dry powdered milk
1 tbsp butter or oil
¼ cup potato flakes

1. Mix all ingredients into large bowl and mix into a smooth ball.
2. Let rise until double – 1 to 1 ½ hours. Punch down and let rise again. Let rise a third time, punch down, and then shape into loaf or rolls. Let rise again until double and bake.

High altitude: Decrease yeast and vinegar to ½ Tablespoon each

*Landra's recipe note – Vinegar is a surprisingly common ingredient in baked goods, considering that it has such a sharp flavor. But as an acid, vinegar is often included in cake and cookie batters to react with baking soda and start the chemical reaction needed to produce carbon dioxide and give those batters a lift as they bake.

Pizza Dough/Bread Sticks
2 ½ cups medium hot water
5 tsp SAF instant yeast*
2 tbsp sugar
3 tbsp oil
1 t. Salt
6 cups flour (half AP and half wheat or 100% whole wheat)
1 to 2 cubes of butter

1. Pour medium hot water in mixing bowl.
2. Sprinkle yeast on top and allow to dissolve.
3. Add sugar, salt, and oil.
4. Gradually add approximately 6 cups of flour.
5. Melt 1-2 cubes butter on cookie sheet in oven as it is heating to (up to) 300 degrees and melt in (Solar) oven.
6. Place dough on cookie sheet and press to fill pan, make sure butter gets on top of the dough.
7. Allow to double in size (About 10-15 minutes)
8. Bake until desired browning is accomplished. Cut into strips or top with favorite pizza toppings.

* When using regular yeast change amount to 2 Tbsp.

Candied Carrots
1 quart canned jar of carrots or 2 store bought 15 oz. cans
2 tbsp butter
¼ - ½ cups brown sugar
1 tsp cinnamon

dash of nutmeg
¼ tsp salt

1. Drain carrots
2. In a pot, melt butter and add the rest of the ingredients. Gently cook until the sugar had dissolved.
3. Add carrots and mix until they are glazed.

Chocolate Cake
1 ½ cup AP flour
1 cup sugar
¼ cup cocoa powder
1 tsp baking soda
½ tsp salt
1/3 cup oil
1 tsp vanilla extract
1 tsp white Vinegar
1 cup water

1. Preheat oven to 350 degrees F (175 degrees C). Lightly grease one 9x5 inch loaf pan.
2. Sift together the flour, sugar, cocoa, baking soda and salt. Add the oil, vanilla, vinegar and water. Mix together until smooth.
3. Pour into prepared pan and bake at 350 degrees F (175 degrees C) for 45 minutes.
4. Remove from oven and allow to cool.

Raspberry Squares
½ cup butter or margarine (at room temperature)
1 cup light brown sugar, firmly packed
1 cup oats (Quick Cook or Old Fashioned)
1 tsp baking powder
½ tsp almond extract
1 cup AP flour
½ cup raspberry preservatives

1. Preheat oven to 350 degrees. Coat an 8 x 8-inch baking pan with cooking spray.
2. In a medium bowl, cream butter and brown sugar until smooth and fluffy. Mix in almond extract.
3. Mix in flour, baking powder and oats until mixture is combined and crumbly.
4. Reserve 1/4 cup of the mixture for topping; set aside. Pat remaining mixture into the bottom of prepared baking pan.
5. Spoon preserves on top of oat layer, spreading as much as possible without disturbing the bottom layer. Sprinkle reserved topping on the top of preserve layer.
6. Bake for 30 to 40 minutes or until lightly browned.
7. Remove from oven and cool on a wire rack. When cooled, cut into squares.

*Landra's Note: This recipe is perfect to prepare in a Solar Oven.

Butter
Empty Mason Jar
1 8oz. carton Trader Joe's (Shelf Stable) Whipping Cream
¼ t. salt

Add ingredients into Mason Jar and shake vigorously until desired consistency is achieved.

Tomato Sauce
2 (28 ounce) cans tomato puree
1 (28 ounce) can peeled plum tomatoes
2 cloves garlic
1 small onion, diced
6 cloves
1 t.sp basil
1 tsp kosher salt
¼ tsp fresh ground pepper
2 tbsp sugar

¼ cup extra virgin olive oil
¼ cup parmesan cheese

1. In a large pot, sauté onion and garlic in olive oil. Empty plum tomatoes into large bowl and mash with a fork.
2. Add all ingredients to pot and simmer.

Pizza Sauce
2 (6 ounce) cans tomato paste
2 cloves garlic
3 tbsp dried parsley flakes
4 tsp dried onion flakes
1 tsp dried oregano
1 tsp dried basil
2 cup. water

1. Combine tomato paste, garlic, parsley flakes, onion, oregano, basil and water in 2 quart saucepan.
2. Cook over medium high heat until mixture boils.
3. Reduce heat to low and simmer 10 minutes. Cool a little and spread on your pizza crust and proceed with remainder of your toppings.

Roasted Red Pepper Alfredo Sauce
¼ cup flour (whole wheat or all-purpose)
10 tbsp powdered milk
¾ tbsp salt
½ - 1 c up parmesan cheese
2 cups water
½ tsp red pepper flakes (or to taste)
½ jar of roasted red peppers
olive or vegetable oil

Mix dry ingredients together well. Add enough of the liquid to make a smooth paste.
Add to pan over medium heat and add remaining liquid.
Stir frequently until sauce thickens and comes to a boil.

Drain and pat dry roasted red peppers and chop into bite size pieces, add to sauce when sauce is thickened.

Ricotta Cheese

8 cups water
1 ½ cup instant milk
3 tbsp white vinegar
½ tsp salt

1. Place water, milk and salt in large pot on medium high heat. Allow milk to heat up slowly. Stir occasionally.
2. Once you see steam start to form above the surface, stir constantly until it boils.
3. Remove from heat, add the vinegar and stir gently for one minute. Curds will begin forming.
4. Cover and allow it to sit undisturbed for at least 30 minutes
5. Ladle the ricotta into a fine mesh colander (you can also line the colander with cheese cloth.
6. Place the colander (with the ricotta in it) in a larger pan so it can drain.
7. Let it drain for 10+ minutes (depending on how wet/dry you want your cheese).

Chapter 5

Safety and Shelter

Come, my people, enter thou into thy chambers, and shut thy doors about thee: hide thyself as it were for a little moment, until the indignation be overpast.
Isaiah 26:20

Just as The Honorable Minister Louis Farrakhan's words in the beginning of the book spoke of, there will probably come a time when we will have to seek shelter in our homes. So this chapter will discuss the aspects of staying as safe and comfortable as we possibly can while we are seeking shelter indoors. Let's begin with our water supply.

Water borne diseases are a potential problem. This will be discussed in depth in chapter 7, but for right now, unclean water equals a big problem. We all know that our bodies can only be without water for a few days, so water supplies will be the first felt impact; therefore great care must be taken to properly purify water before drinking. Most of us have experienced this first hand and observed that water supplies will be one of the first items that we see disappear from the shelves of stores.

So we must take great care in learning how to properly purify drinking water BEFORE drinking it. Sanitation goes hand in hand with purifying water, so we will discuss that a little later in this chapter, but until then, here are methods of purifying our water.

Purifying Water

Boiling
The easiest way to purify water is to boil it, provided you have the equipment to do so. Meaning you will have to use your emergency stove if your electricity and or gas are off. Bring water in a pot to a boil over high heat until you have rolling bubbles, and let them roll for at least five minutes. Don't forget to let it cool down before drinking.

Disinfect
You can use household liquid bleach (regular household bleach contains 5.25% sodium chloride) to kill microorganisms. Please do not use scented, color-safe or bleaches with added cleaners, only regular plain bleach.
Add 16 drops of bleach per gallon of water, stir and let stand for 30 minutes. If the water doesn't have a slight bleach odor, repeat the dosage and let stand another 15 minutes.

Again - the only agent used to purify water should be household liquid bleach.

Filtration or purification pumps

Ok, so now we are getting a little fancy with the purification. Many camping stores stock various pumps with filters and purifiers to make sure non-potable water goes in, but drinkable water comes out — right into your water bottle. This is done through a process of squeezing water through ceramic or charcoal filter and treating it with chemicals.
Some hi-tech water bottles have this process built into them, so that you don't need to pump water into a separate one; the purification process happens as you squeeze or suck water directly into your mouth. If your funds allow for it, each member of your family can have their own bottle.

Purification drops and tablets

A simple and inexpensive — but not necessarily the best tasting — method of purifying wild water is by dropping in a couple of purification tablets or drops. The most common chemical used is iodine, but chlorine or potassium permanganate is also effective. Let the chemicals treat the water for at least 20 minutes before consuming, and mix it with powdered mixes to mask any of its taste. If you are drinking plain water, there will be a chemical after taste.

Distillation

Fill a pot halfway with water. Tie a cup to the handle on the pot's lid so that the cup will hang right side up when the lid is upside-down. Make sure the cup is not dangling in the water. Boil the water for 20 minutes. The water that drips from the lid to the cup is distilled. This is my last choice because it is time consuming and does not produce a great deal of drinkable water.

Safest Areas in The House

The first and most important thing to find is a safe area in the house: an interior room. Remember that you will need to stay inside and away from windows, skylights and doors, especially glass doors. This room should be one such as a closet or bathroom and preferably on the lower level. Now, the key to this room truly being a 'Safe Room' is that it should be stocked with a survival bag specifically designated for this room and filled with items that you would need to remain sheltered inside for several hours. My suggestions are as follows:

- Battery-powered radio
- Flashlight
- Extra batteries
- Battery powered or cellular phone (if no phone in room)
- Snack foods
- Water or drinks
- Plastic sheeting for windows, doors, air vents or other opening, which are already pre-cut and labeled
- Rolls of duct tape for the plastic sheeting
- Towel for under the door
- First Aid Kit

Keep in mind that if flooding is a threat, your safe room cannot be located on the lowest level! Also, remember to turn off the electricity at the main breaker.

A bit of a side bar here, in the event that your home loses power, turn off the major appliances such as the air conditioner and water heater to reduce damage. But even before there is a power outage it is important to follow these few guidelines:

- Do not use electrical appliances, including your computer.
- Do not go outside.
- Once the eye of the storm passes over you, there will be a short period of quiet and calm. But remember

that the other side of the storm will soon come, and you can be hit/injured by debris. *Re-watch the movie, The Day After Tomorrow to jar your memory.
- Beware of lightning.
- Don't use the phone or take a bath/shower during the storm

Ok, I am inspired here to make a confession, growing up I used to get yelled at during storms for standing at the front door, yes with the door open and being mesmerized at the power of storms. I became very good at seemingly tuning out my mother's voice as she fussed, "Landra, close that door before you get struck by lightning." I would stand there saying "WooooooW" My point is: do as I say, not as I do. (smile)

Warm Weather

Imagine this: its July 12th, the middle of summer, blazing hot and POOF! There it is, a power outage! No air conditioner or fan and the utilities companies are reporting that the power will be out for the next few days. What do you do? How will you stay cool?

- Heat rises, so retreat to the lowest level of your home. Surprisingly, your basement can be from 10 to 15 degrees cooler than the rest of your home.
- Do not create additional heat. These suggestions are basic, but turn off the lights and do your cooking outside. Under no circumstances should you turn on the oven or stove and take only cool showers.
- Limit your consumption of caffeine and eat cool foods.
- During the day when it's hotter outside, keep your windows closed and your blinds and curtains drawn. Black-out curtains pinned over the windows will help keep all of the sunlight out. If you don't have black out curtains, you can use aluminum foil over your windows. It will deflect the suns heat away from your windows – think of your car visor.

- Wear the proper clothing

Cold Weather

All right, I would so rather be too hot than too cold. So what do we do on January 30th and that ice storm has just caused a now heavy tree to break on an electricity wire and snapped it? That's right, your power is out and because the roads look like an ice-skating rink, the roads are impassible, aka, no power trucks are coming to turn on the lights. And worse than the lights, the heat in your home is supplied by electricity and yes, your house is getting colder and colder.

- Wear the proper clothing. Wear a hat and cover your feet. This will help you to maintain your body heat.
- Make sure your home is properly insulated. If necessary, insulate walls and attic. This will help you to conserve electricity and reduce your home's power demands for heat. Caulk and weather-strip doors and windowsills to keep cold air out, allowing the inside temperature to stay warmer longer.
- Install storm windows or cover windows with plastic from the inside. This will provide an extra layer of insulation, keeping more cold air out.
- Instead of trying to heat the whole house, focus your attention on heating just one room of the house. Everyone's body heat in one room is a great help to keeping everyone warm. Try to pick a room that gets a lot of natural sunlight and has a heating source. Ideally, you would pick a windowed room on the southwest side of your home.
- Consider keeping safe emergency heating equipment:

    (a) Fireplace with ample supply of wood.
    (b) Small, well-vented wood, coal, or camp stove with fuel.
    (c) Portable space heater or kerosene heater. Use only the correct fuel for your unit and follow the manufacturer's instructions.

Refuel outdoors only, and only when cool. **Keep your kerosene heater at least three feet away from furniture and other flammable objects.**

(d) When using alternative heat from a fireplace, wood stove, space heater, etc., **use fire safeguards and ventilate properly.** Fire hazard is greatly increased in the winter because alternate heating sources are used without following proper safety precautions.

Sanitation

Proper sanitation is a subject that is often ignored in emergency preparedness and all the preparation in the world can crumble if you become ill. After a calamity, we could be faced with weeks of sanitary problems. And traditionally the lack of sanitation facilities following major disaster can bring serious health risks. So, the proper steps must be taken to avoid post disaster illness.

If the disaster includes rain, keep in mind that flood waters may contain fecal material from overflowing sewage systems, so there is always a risk of disease from eating or drinking anything contaminated with flood water. Additionally, there is a great possibility of a shortage of water supply coupled with broken water lines. And if the untreated sewage polluted the water supply, people will quickly become ill or perish. With basic health care and sanitation all but destroyed and high numbers of survivor's likely left homeless, unchecked infectious disease and contamination will pose a threat to survivors. This is what took place in Haiti after their major earthquake. Many people developed Cholera.

KEEP YOUR HANDS CLEAN

Here is a portable hand washing station. A water jug, bungee cords, a paper towel holder, paper towels, hand soap and a wash bin on the ground to catch the excess water.

Even though some diseases are spread by sewage it is not the only way that it can spread. Consider that just because an emergency occurs, does not mean that our digestive system stops taking its course. Do you understand what I mean? Our need to get rid of human waste will continue. It is crucial that we take a few simple steps to properly handle this type of sanitation. Don't forget, one of the last things that you want to deal with is becoming ill during this time, as disasters might equate to having less available medical care options! The medical professionals just might be busy dealing with their own problems at home. And hospitals might be using generators and have only a limited staff available.

Depending on where you live in the country will best determine what type of option can be used to best suit your needs. But before building an emergency toilet you want to follow some simple rules.

When creating an emergency toilet, it is important to:

- Locate the toilet away from food preparation or eating areas (refer back to chapter 4)
- Locate latrines and portable toilets at least 100 feet away from surface water bodies such as lakes, rivers, streams, and at least 100 feet downhill or away from any drinking water source (well or spring), home, apartment, or campsite.
- Provide a place close to the emergency toilet to wash hands that offers soap, running water (or hand sanitizer) and paper towels – your portable hand washing station.

Continue To Use The Toilet
Unless you have running water, using your water supply to fill the toilet reservoir with water **will not** be an option. However, with the use of trash bags, you should be able to use the toilet within your home and remove the waste

at a later time. The idea here is to place the bag in the toilet, and once finished, seal the bag until next use.

This method brings to mind another important factor, keeping the odor down. Although we are accustomed to being able to flush the toilet any time we feel like, try to think of this situation as if living in a Recreational Vehicle or while out camping. Yes there is a level of 'roughing' it, but there are chemicals available to help keep the odor down as well as breaking down toilet tissue left behind in the plastic bag. Often used is sawdust and a product called Quicklime (Calcium Oxide). Traditionally, Quicklime is used in water and sewage treatment to reduce acidity, to harden, as a flocculant (a substance added to a suspension to enhance aggregation of the suspended particles) and to remove phosphates and other impurities.

Bucket
There are several options to help us keep the waste either out of the home completely or covered with a lid. One of the advantages of using a bucket is the option of sealing it

with a lid. The lid will help keep the smell in and the insects out.

AN IMPORTANT NOTE ABOUT INSECTS AND FECES

If a fly happens touch the feces and then lands on your food, you could have a recipe for illness. So keep the lid closed to keep the flies and other insects away!!! And maintain a safe distance between your toilet and cooking areas.

Now, back to the bucket toilet - line it with 2 of the same style garbage bags. For added comfort a couple of short length 2 x 4s, or even better a commercially produced top made just for that purpose on top. *See the chapter 8 for websites that have this type of toilet seat available for sale. Lastly, use some sand, dirt, **kitty litter**, or even quicklime along with some bleach solution before and after the bucket is used. Replace after a few uses.

Latrine

A Latrine is a communal space with multiple toilets designed for human waste. It can be as simple as a hole dug into the ground to collect human waste.

This hole in ground is a real as it might get depending upon your location.

Chapter 6

Thinking About Our Family, Friends and Neighbors

Children will take their lead from the behavior of their parents, media and other adults around. If you have a level of calmness, so will they! If you are panicking, ie. not prepared, you can expect, in most cases, children to respond with anxiety, fear and possibly confusion. The more prepared your children are, potentially the calmer they will be.

Years ago I owned a in-home day care center, and at least once a week I would teach my students, aged 2-5 years old about disaster preparedness and even have drills which included my students stopping whatever it was that they were engaged in and seeking safety under a table. Granted when we first began, the children ran around and laughed for most of the drill, but over time and with continued teaching they all became calmer and the drills ran very smoothly. Additionally, I used to show them age appropriate videos which included natural disasters and the effects of them, along with teaching about atmospheric subjects such as rain, hail, snow and even the effects of earthquakes. In turn, they would go home and talk to their parents about preparedness. The parents would often come to me and make jokes about tornadoes and earthquakes, but at least I knew that they knew that I was teaching useful subjects to their children. (smile)

Lastly, children can be much stronger than you might give them credit for, so practice your family plan and with your supervision show them videos of natural disasters. This can lessen the shock if and when the real thing hits home. See chapter 8 for a list of training materials that you can use to prepare your little ones.

Elderly

Senior citizens, especially those with limited mobility and or medical issues are extremely vulnerable during disasters. My experience during Hurricane Sandy included dealing with one of my favorite relatives, who happens to be my 90 something, year old Great Aunt Nan. Before the storm, I visited with her to make sure that she was safe and secure with basic supplies. She simply smiled at me and informed me that the news was making a big deal out of a little rain that we were going to have and that she was fine. Well, two days after the storm when I returned to her home, I found her sitting in the kitchen in a dark house. As most people in the area, she had lost her electricity. I quickly drove to my house, grabbed as many power outage lights that I could spare (flashlights and candles) and then returned to her home. She was so thankful for the lights, but not thankful enough to agree to come with me out of her home. With that beautiful smile of hers, she told me that she was not leaving and that "The Lord" was going to take care of her. In the most animated motion that I could muster up, I slowly looked over to my right shoulder, followed by looking to my left and then looked her in the face without cracking a smile and said "Yes Aunt Nan, the Lord is *gonna* help you. He sent me here to get you, now let's go!" She all but laughed herself out of the chair, and then told me that I was sweet but she wasn't going anywhere.

Ok, so the story is funny now, after the fact, but at that moment, I was very upset. It did however teach me a valuable lesson, and that is that seniors more often than not, are grounded where they are. Change is difficult and even more so during stressful times, such as during and after disasters.

Visually impaired

Just as senior citizens, visually impaired people might be extremely reluctant to leave familiar surroundings after a disaster. Imagine how you would feel if someone that you are not familiar asks you to evacuate. Even a trained guide dog could become confused or disoriented in a disaster. Remember, people who are blind or partially sighted may have to depend on others to lead them, as well as their dog, to safety during a disaster.

Hearing impaired

Those hard of hearing will need to make special arrangements to receive warnings. The National Weather System offers non-verbal information imbedded in its broadcasts which provide warnings of life threatening events to the hearing impaired community. Some of their receivers are equipped with special output connectors that activate alerting devices such as vibrators, bed shakers, pillow vibrators, strobe lights and other alerting systems.

Mobility impaired

The immobile may need assistance to get to a shelter or help evacuating their homes. Additionally, it must be taken into consideration that elevators are not to be used for evacuation unless directed to do so by the fire department or rescue personnel, so if you live on a floor higher than the ground flood, this is something of high importance.

Lastly, during Hurricane Katrina, one of the reasons that some people could not leave the city was because they did not have transportation out of harm's way. So even if you are without a vehicle, you just might fall under the category of being mobility impaired. Make arrangements for transportation today. Come on people, get to know one another. Your life may depend on it!

Single working parent

Single parents may need help to plan for disasters and emergencies regarding school aged children. If one of your neighbors happens to be a working parent, have a conversation and ask them about their plans during an emergency/ disaster. Offer your assistance. Someone else's life may depend on it.

Non-English speaking persons

Foreign language speakers may need assistance planning for and responding to emergencies too. Community and cultural groups must plan a key role in helping to keep people informed. Therefore, take serious consideration to know the people in your neighborhood. There is nothing wrong with learning a few phrases in various languages related to assistance. Believe me, if you ask any 4 year old, how do you say help me in Spanish, because of the television show, Dora The Explorer, they will answer AYUADAME!

People with special dietary needs

Special foods may be more costly for the average person. However, one must take special precautions to have an adequate emergency food and medical supply in such cases. As well as making sure that family and neighbors are also aware of their medical conditions. Many years ago when I first became serious with my disaster preparedness planning, I remember sitting at the kitchen table with my mother and making "rescue" plans for my 6 great aunts and uncles that lived within a 5 mile radius of our home. Unbeknownst to them, my mother and I reviewed all of the various illnesses that they each suffered from and shopped for food and supplies that we thought they would need if a disaster took place that they would be forced to stay with us. Granted, only one of the 6 ever needed to be rescued and she refused, but it's the thought that counts right?! (smile) Seriously, this type of thinking was brought on because my father was a long term diabetic so we always needed to maintain certain foods and medications in the house.

People with medical conditions

This goes hand in hand with special dietary needs. If you are suffering from certain medical conditions, you should know the location and availability of more than one facility if dependent on a dialysis machine or other life-sustaining equipment or treatment. And if possible, have access to portable machines at home. Remember, even if you can't afford all of your supplies, some preparation is better than not preparation at all.

Women

In terms of a women's needs during a disaster, a supply of sanitary napkins is probably something that most women might not think about until the time comes when it is needed, so please make sure that you have an ample supply of sanitary napkins, along with any other month supplies that you are accustom to using, ie. Advil, etc. Disasters can cause stress induced changes in the cycle of a women's menstrual flow. A Pregnant Woman and Women with younger children need to factor in the amounts of baby formula that might be needed, if the child is not being breastfed. Remember, even when being breastfed, stress can cause changes in the breast.

If you have a baby or toddler and need to evacuate - don't waste precious space by trying to carry a stroller. Shirts, towels and small blankets sheets can be used to carry a baby.

People with intellectual disabilities and Dementia

Mentally handicapped persons may need help responding to emergencies and travelling to a shelter. They may not completely understand what is happening and become confused or even violent. Understanding how to prepare major disasters is a matter of life and death. So in the words of Arsenio Hall – "Let's get busy."

Even though the information listed above is speaking to specific groups, the name of this chapter is Thinking about our family, neighbors and friends. One of greatest assets that we have for our survival is each other. But always remember, (Allah) God is the Greatest and to Him do we seek refuge and mercy to survive the fall of America.

Chapter 7

I've Weathered the Storm - So What's Next?

Congratulations, you made it through the storm, so let's get to the aftermath. Well, the first thing that you will probably notice is that you don't have any electricity. This you will soon learn has a trickledown effect much larger than not having lights in your home.

If the power outage is widespread and long-lasting, and oftimes it is, there may be no working gas pumps in your area. So if you want to retain mobility, it is a good practice to try not to ever let your vehicle's gas tank get lower than a ½ tank.

Right after Hurricane Sandy, I found myself waiting in line for a little less than a half tank of gas for over 3 hours. Don't feel badly for me, because I was prepared to wait. On my passenger side front seat I had my charged up cell phone, a portable tv, the daily newspaper, something to drink and a toasted cream cheese wheat bagel. The Police were also at the gas station. They were directing traffic to maintain some order and make sure that the gas stations policy of $40 maximum was obeyed. This gas station along this the highly traveled highway that I was on, Route 17 in northern New Jersey, was open serving gas. At this point, about 4 days after the hurricane had passed, almost all of the other gas stations were either out of gas or simply unable to pump the gas because of the power outage. Most people didn't realize that many gas stations do not have emergency generators, so when the power goes out, so does the availability to pump gas. Because I had started out before the storm with a ¾ full gas tank, my $40 gasoline max was perfect to cap of my trucks' gas tank.

Guess what also doesn't work during a blackout, ATMs and neither do cash registers, so keep a supply of cash in small bills handy that you may be able to purchase supplies, if you can find a store that's open that is. It's best to have small bills in case exact payment is needed and the store doesn't have change available. Can you imagine paying $20 for a loaf of bread because the store didn't have change! So don't forget your small bills, $1's and $5s. Before leaving your home, try calling around to major retailers if you're in a pinch for supplies. Some stores, including most big box retailers, have actually installed backup generators and are able to continue operating during a blackout.

By the way, if you are feeling completely in need of some electronics and you desperately need to recharge small items such as your portable television, iPod or cellphones, you can use an inverter plugged into the cigarette lighter to recharge via the car's battery. Don't get carried away, though (especially in the winter) because you can drain the battery to the point that your car won't start.. And don't forget that non-electrical entertainment can be a lifesaver when the power outage stretches from hours into days. Board games, cards, books, comics and coloring books can help fend off boredom for both adults and kids.

If you live in a town or city, most likely stop-lights will not be working or blinking. Treat every intersection like it is a four-way stop sign! I once had to drive in the dark over to my cousin Shelley's house during a power outage. The word frightening isn't even close to what I experienced. Though she only lived a town over, driving on a pitch black road in a township is completely different that a pitch black country road.

Ok, before we talk about communications, I need to mention that you will need to prepare your mind to not go MAD from the *eerie* silence. If you are living in a city, you might hear some people outside talking; however, if you are in the suburbs you probably will only hear silence. You will then realize that absence of the hum of electricity; the refrigerator, your computer, etc. So your mind must keep busy. I addition to my books and board games, I also have a small MP3 player of containing music and positive lectures. And on to the subject of communications we go.

You have probably already experienced this in the past, but I will say it anyway, your telephone and cell phone will probably not work properly. It is better to send a text message than attempting a phone call because texting uses less bandwidth than a telephone call. If you attempt a call and receive an all circuits busy message, you should then try to call your out of state contact that will then call whomever you are trying to reach across town. It might sound a little strange, but it actually works!

If you have a landline phone, fantastic because it has a greater chance of working unless the phone lines have been damaged. Oh, this reminds me, if remove the 'bundle' that you have from that internet company. Granted, you may save a little money having your internet, cable and telephone all bundled together HOWEVER, if there is a storm and one goes out - then THEY ALL GO OUT!!! Keep your landline phone separate using a traditional telephone company. Additionally, have a landline phone that does not require electricity. Keep one that plugs directly into the wall. Yes, an old school telephone is what you need.

While we are talking about old school, let's take it all the way back to having your telephone numbers memorized and start using a phone book again. Smart phones have made us quite dumb. When your smartphone dies, if you do not have important numbers memorized you will be out of luck.

Other methods of communication include:

- Walkie Talkies
- Multi Use Radio Service (MURS)
- General Mobile Radio Service (GMRS)
- Ham Radio

If you are in distress, there are a few actions that communicate distress such as a flare or an upside down flag.

In chapter 1 it was mentioned that during a massive 2003 power outage that most of the television stations didn't' work, so there is always a chance that local media will not be available. We also have talked previously about the lack of running water which causes problems with Sanitation, so please refer back to chapter 5.

Time Management will be a key factor in how you plan your days. You might need to change your schedule around so that you can complete all of your assignments before it becomes dark. As an example, during a power outage, I found myself cooking my dinner at 10:30am so that I could eat around 12-2. I was then able to use able to use the light of the sun, not having to waste candles during the daytime. It's a small thing, but its best to use your free light (daytime) while its available.

Lastly, the trickle-down effect caused by disasters is HUGE, especially in relation to income. The cycle of generating income can be interrupted but your bills and daily expenses don't stop. Unless you own a Home Depot or Lowes, you are not going to make a quick recovery. Preceding a severe weather condition often hundreds of schools, offices, malls, airports and restaurants must close their doors in anticipation. So think about it, if businesses are closed, the lack of revenue trickles down to its employees not working. This further trickle down will cause you to have less spendable income while the bills remain constant. Believe me, I have experienced this and it is real and a horrible feeling. During my time running my day care center, my rule of thumb was if I was open and available to work, the parents were responsible for payment, yes, even if the child did not attend. However, if I was not available to care for children, then I had to take the financial lose. Well, I certainly could not open the center without power in my home. The long story short is no work equals no income.

I sometimes enjoy watching disaster type movies, and while taking a break one day during the writing of this chapter, I came across a movie on Netflix called Goodbye World. My husband and I watched in awe as we viewed the characters react during a power outage inspired apocalyptic event. Other than the college reunion theme woven into the storyline, there were some very critical lessons to be learned from that movie. I suggest that you watch that movie as well as those listed below. They all have something that can be learned from watching and studying. And if you are still desirous of watching and studying a few more movies, check out:
((http://www.disasterflicks.com/natural-disaster-movies.html))
for a more complete list of movies!

- The Day After Tomorrow
- Day After Tomorrow
- Dante's Peak
- Goodbye World
- The Great Los Angeles Earthquake

Lastly, although not a movie, also please watch Minister Farrakhan's 52 week Time and What Must Be Done Lecture Series. ((http://www.noi.org/thetime/))

Chapter 8

God Helps Those That Help Themselves

Remember in the first chapter when I wrote, NOBODY IS COMING TO SAVE YOU? Well, I stand by that statement, they are not coming BUT there is something that you can get from them now ...Free online and in person training. Reading this book is only phase I of preparation.

In addition there must be a hands-on element, so come on modern day Noah, start building your ark with food, supplies and key essential survival kits as I have sighted in this book. (smile)

Ok, let's start with FEMA. They offer will over 100 free online courses, many of which can be located here: http://www.training.fema.gov/

If you are attend a religious or community group you might consider organizing a neighborhood CERT group. CERT stands for Community Emergency Response Team. The training that I took was free and at the end of the 6 week class, I was gifted with a duffle bag full of FREE supplies. http://www.ready.gov/citizen-corps

Red Cross
Offers dozens of courses, most of them however, are not free. They do offer nice variations of classes though. Such as: in person, online and blended. So you might want to take a look at their site.
http://www.redcross.org/take-a-class

Salvation Army Emergency Disaster Services Training Program offers several free online courses for those working within the Salvation Army Organization. The link to one of the courses is listed below.

http://centralusa.salvationarmy.org/usc/national_eds_progra
m

The Centers For Disease Control offers quite a few very interesting courses such as Bioterrorism, Mass Casualties, Radiation and Chemical Emergencies. Their available courses can be found here:
http://www.cdc.gov/

The National Center For Disaster Preparedness falls under the umbrella of Columbia university and offers more than 40 **free** online courses are to help public health workers, and even though I do not work in the field of health, I have taken a few of these courses and found then to be extremely helpful. Their website shares this about their courses:

- All Courses are FREE.

- Most courses have multiple lessons which allow a learner to complete a course at their own pace. However, each lesson must be completed in order.

- After completing a course including passing the post-test and course survey, you will automatically receive an e-mail containing a certificate of completion.

- This enhanced system will meet all of your education and training needs, including tracking activity and keeping records of courses completed and in progress.
http://ncdp.columbia.edu/

Coursea also offers a class on Disaster Preparedness. This interesting course is taught by Professor Michael Beach from the University of Pittsburgh, and he shares with the students his strong views on maintaining a winning attitude regarding disasters.

The Content listed on the course website is:

- The Disaster Cycle and its evolution
- Personal preparedness
- Communication
- Security
- Supplies and other stuff
- Shelter, Food and Water
- Comfort
- Preparedness on the level of institutions and governments
- Ethical considerations including Justice and the distribution of resources, Utilitarianism, and personal responsibility
- Examples and realities from disaster response such as Memorial Hospital after Hurricane Katrina and personal experiences from the faculty Attitude and Awareness

https://www.coursera.org/course/disasterprep

Back to **FEMA** we go. They offer a great deal of FREE preparedness training for children using games and downloads. The information is age appropriate and will hold a child's attention.
http://www.ready.gov/kids

For your youngest of children, it doesn't get better than watching the cute and loveable Grover from **Sesame Street** teach aspects of Disaster Preparedness. There are also downloads available on this website.
http://www.sesamestreet.org/parents/topicsandactivities/tool kits/ready

The Disaster Resistant Communities Group offers a 28 part Hearing Impaired Training.
http://www.drc-group.com/project/jitt-hi.html

I advise you to reach out to older relatives and neighbors. Chances are great that you know someone that knows how to can, and whom can teach you this lost art. And believe me, they will be delighted, but in the event that you do not have any someone that can teach you how to can, the National Center for Home Food Preservation offers FREE and self-paced online lessons for those who would like to learn more about home canning and preservation.

Their topics include:
- Introduction to Food Preservation
- General Canning
- Canning Acid Foods
- Canning Low-Acid Foods

https://spock.fcs.uga.edu/ext/food/nchfp_elc/

For those that would like to attend a class in person, below is a list of local extension offices that offers information on canning throughout the United States
http://www.freshpreserving.com/community/classes

And if you were wondering, what exactly is an Extension Office? Well Wikipedia states that "Extension Office is a general term meaning the application of scientific research and new knowledge to agricultural practices through farmer education. The field of 'extension' now encompasses a wider range of communication and learning activities organized for rural people by educators from different disciplines, including agriculture, agricultural marketing, health, and business studies."

Each state has an Emergency Management Agency, so do your individual research and register for any FREE courses that they may offer as well as their alert systems. As an example, the State of New York has organized the New York State Citizens Prepared Corps, and list of their available training classes can be accessed at.

http://www.dhses.ny.gov/aware-prepare/nysprepare/

And an example of a townships alert system can be seen here in Teaneck, New Jersey.
http://www.teanecknj.gov/index.cfm?fuseaction=home.subscriptions

Following certain Twitter accounts is also good idea. Subscriptions to your County, Township, and Weather Channel-Break News will provide you an abundance of local and national news.

Lastly, ask your local city hall for a copy of the Disaster Preparedness Plan for the township.

Well, that's it. I am prayerful that after reading through this book that you will work diligently to put a plan and kit together, and even bigger than that, share the information that you have learned with all of your loved one and neighbors. Organize your friends, family and communities. Let us pray and then work to try to save ourselves during this great Fall. I again advise you to watch the series, The Time And What Must Be Done, given by the Honorable Minister Louis Farrakhan. His words might better help you understand the urgency of our actions during this dangerous hour.
http://www.noi.org/thetime/

May God (Allah) guide you, me and us to do what is right.

Acknowledgements

It is truly a blessing to have people in your life that help you to grow and help in the discovery of gifts, talents and even defects.(smile) Others sometimes are just there to give us a kind work at the right time. The following people all fit into one of the above categories. Special Thank You

The Honorable Minister Louis Farrakhan, thank you so much for your hard work: teaching the masses of people the teachings of the Most Honorable Elijah Muhammad and making me to understand the importance of preparedness. Mother Tynnetta Muhammad, thank you for allowing me the honor of traveling and learning from you and yes, I do understand how go-bags are extremely important! Brother Jabril Muhammad and his wife Dr. Patina Muhammad, thank you for sharing with me guidance on various important subjects.(smile) Brother Wahid Muhammad, thank you for you constant encouragement and now let's start working on the next project!

Thank you to some of my amazing cousins Geralean Jones, Shelley Silverman, Lisa Samuels, Wayne Fisher. Oh my goodness gracious, you all have helped me to weather soooo many storms, I LOVE YOU all dearly.   Thank you Hafeez Muhammad, Johnna Muhammad and my Muhammad Mosque #7 (NYC) family. Thank you Englewood NJ Study Group, especially Sister Harriet Muhammad. Thank you to the believers at my family church, Mount Calvary Baptist Church (Englewood, NJ), and the believers at my down south family church Sandhill Baptist Church (Kershaw, SC). Thank you Dr. Ridgley and Anne Mu'min Muhammad of Muhammad Farms for allowing me the opportunity to speak on the MOA Blog Talk radio show to share disaster preparedness tips.

My special study buddies, Kadara Muhammad (Rochester, NY), Giselle Muhammad (Bermuda) Joyce and

Bobby Muhammad (Colorado Springs, CO). Not only did you all give me encouragement and constructive advice, you also helped with the proofing and editing. How blessed I am to know such brilliant minds!

Thank you Phyllis Muhammad (Brooklyn, NY), Nayyirah Muhammad (St. Petersburg, FL) and Sheila Muhammad (Winston Salem, NC) for always having positive words of encouragement for me!

Thank you Corey Muhammad, Keri-Anne Muhammad and Kimberly Muhammad (Charlotte) for understanding that I needed to *disappear*, while working on this book. Thank you Audrey Muhammad, publisher of Virtue Magazine for being the queen of encouragement and a true sister to me. And can't forget your 'mini-me', my niece Hasana Muhammad for all of her tween excitement and encouragement. Thank you to my first nieces Jada and Jasmine Figueroa, I pray that this information will be useful to you both. And a special thank you to my husband, Rasheed L. Muhammad for his constant support, confidence and help with the formatting of this book … LOVE YOU MUCH BLACK MAN!

Lastly, even though my parents are no longer physically alive, I still must acknowledge Bobby Joe Harris and Hortense Samuel-Harris.